MW01226952

TREESOFHOPE

Rise: A Parent's Guide To Sexual Abuse Prevention And Child Safety

Copyright © 2021 by Trees of Hope

Published by Trees of Hope

    3901 West Broward Blvd., #122195,

    Fort Lauderdale, FL 33312

Email booksales@treesofhope.org for any further information for bulk orders or any special requests.

All rights reserved. No part of this publication may be reproduced, stored in or introduced into a retrieval system, or transmitted, in any form, or by any means (electrical, mechanical, photocopying, recording, or otherwise) without the prior written permission of the publisher. Any person who does any unauthorized act in relation to this publication may be liable to criminal prosecution and civil claims for damages.

Cover and interior design: Nicole Escobar

First printing 2021

Printed in the United States of America

Print ISBN: 978-1-7367546-0-3

LIBRARY OF CONGRESS PUBLISHER'S CATALOGING-IN-PUBLICATION DATA

Names: Trees of Hope (Organization) | Escobar, Nicole, designer.

Title: *Rise: a parent's guide to sexual abuse prevention and child safety* / written by Trees of Hope; designed by Nicole Escobar.

Description: Fort Lauderdale, FL: Trees of Hope, [2021] | Includes index.

Identifiers: ISBN: 978-1-7367546-0-3

Subjects: LCSH: Child sexual abuse--Prevention. | Child sexual abuse--Prevention--Study and teaching (Preschool) | Situational awareness--Study and teaching (Preschool) | Sexually abused children--Identification. | Interviewing in child abuse. | Child molesters--Identification. | Online sexual predators--Identification. | Touch--Moral and ethical aspects | Child welfare. | Sexually abused children--Services for.

Classification: LCC: HV6570 .R57 2021 | DDC: 362.76--dc23

Rise

A PARENT'S GUIDE TO SEXUAL ABUSE PREVENTION AND CHILD SAFETY

WRITTEN BY TREES OF HOPE
DESIGNED BY NICOLE ESCOBAR

PUBLISHED BY

TREESOFHOPE

01

WHAT *is* SEXUAL ABUSE?

02

WHY *do* WE NEED SEXUAL ABUSE TRAINING?

03

WHY *do* PEOPLE SEXUALLY ABUSE?

04

PATTERNS *of* SEXUAL ABUSE OFFENDERS

Welcome

WHO IS TREES OF HOPE?

Research shows that approximately 25% of the U.S. population has experienced sexual abuse at some point in their lives. Victims of childhood sexual abuse are far more likely to struggle with addiction, eating disorders, suicidal thoughts, and other destructive behaviors, and may even end up becoming abusers themselves. While the statistics are shocking and the effects disturbing, there is hope! Experts agree that 95% of childhood sexual abuse is preventable through education and training. That is where Trees of Hope comes in.

Trees of Hope was founded in 2006 by a sexual abuse survivor. Since that time, we have impacted thousands of people's lives through our prevention workshops and healing studies. While we are humbled by what we've accomplished so far, there is still so much to be done. Children need to be protected from becoming victims in the future, and survivors need to heal from the wounds of their past. Trees of Hope will not stop until the scourge of sexual abuse has been completely and permanently eradicated from our world.

We have created this *Rise* magazine to help you with one of your most important jobs - to protect your children. But the reality is that you can't be with them 24 hours a day. *Rise* gives you the strategies you need to educate and empower your children to protect themselves when you're not around.

Rise is meant for parents, grandparents, teachers, and other caregivers. *Rise* teaches you awareness strategies for you to teach your children without making them afraid, as well as what to do when facing dangerous or uncomfortable situations.

After reading this magazine, we encourage you to share it with your family, friends, co-workers, and neighbors. In doing so, you will be partnering with us as we fight to end sexual abuse in our community and beyond. We can't do this without you!

EVERY 8 MINUTES

A Child in America Is Sexually Abused

—

Children have a unique outlook on the world around them - they are innocent, trusting, happy, free-spirited, and full of life. This outlook and zest for life can be shattered if the child is a victim of sexual abuse.

DEFENDING THE INNOCENT

As adults, we have a responsibility to prevent sexual abuse from happening to any child. The best way to do this is to learn the signs of child sexual abuse and speak out before a child is victimized.

The truth is, you probably know someone who was sexually abused. It is estimated that over 300,000 children are sexually abused every year, and 1 in 5 adults report being sexually abused as children. With proper education, such as reading this magazine, you are taking the much needed steps to make this world safer for children.

NICOLE ESCOBAR
EXECUTIVE DIRECTOR - nicoleescobar@treesofhope.org

01

WHAT IS CHILD SEXUAL ABUSE?

By age 18, 1 in 3 girls and 1 in 6 boys will be sexually abused.

90% of them will be abused by someone they know, love, and trust.

Child sexual abuse is taking place any time an adult engages in sexual activity with a child. This type of abuse comes in many forms including, but not limited to, rape, sexual assault, exposure, fondling, voyeurism and commercial sexual exploitation. It includes touching and non-touching behaviors. Sometimes, sexual abuse doesn't occur between a child and an adult, but between an older and a younger child.

Child sexual abuse is a crime in all 50 states. It is an epidemic that is severely under reported here in the United States and worldwide. In fact, more than 85 percent of adults who were sexually abused state they did not report it to police or an authority figure.

The *Rise* magazine will provide you with the information you need to help prevent child sexual abuse.

TYPES OF SEXUAL ABUSE

—

Child sexual abuse occurs when a child is persuaded or forced to take place in sexual activity. Physical contact is not necessary for child sexual abuse to occur. In some cases, a child may not understand that what is happening to him or her is abuse or that it is wrong.

CHILD SEXUAL ABUSE FALLS INTO THE FOLLOWING TWO CATEGORIES:

CONTACT (OR TOUCHING) ABUSE

- Encouraging or forcing a child to engage in a sexual activity

- Coercing a child to take his or her clothes off

- Forcing a child to touch someone else's genitals or masturbate

- Penetration or rape by putting a body part or object inside a child's vagina, anus, or mouth

- Sexually touching a child anywhere on the body, whether or not the child is wearing clothes

NON-CONTACT (NON-TOUCHING) ABUSE

- Encouraging or forcing a child to watch or listen to people engage in sexual activity

- Voyeurism - inappropriately watching a child dress or bathe

- Showing a child pictures, video, or internet sites of pornography

- Online abuse involving making, viewing, or distributing child abuse images

- Sexually exploiting a child for money, status, or power

- Sexually grooming and meeting a child with the intent of abusing them

- Asking a child to pose for pictures without their clothes on

CHILD SEXUAL ABUSE: STATS YOU NEED TO KNOW

Many misconceptions surround child sexual abuse. Some widely circulated myths are that child sexual abuse doesn't happen often, only happens to girls, or is only perpetrated by strangers. The following statistics can help you better understand the magnitude and repercussions of child sexual abuse:

- **In 8 out of 10 cases of rape,** the victim knew the perpetrator. [1]

- **Only 12% of child abuse** is ever reported to the authorities. [1]

- **96% of people** who sexually abuse children are male, and **76.8% of people** who sexually abuse children are adults. [1]

- **1 in 4 girls and 1 in 6 boys** will be sexually abused by the age of 18. [1]

- **81% of women and 35% of men** report significant short or long-term impacts such as Post-Traumatic Stress Disorder (PTSD). [1]

- **34% of people** who sexually abuse a child are family members of the child. [1]

  Stats with 1 are from the National Sexual Violence Resource Center.

SEXUAL ABUSE MYTHS

While many facts and statistics can be found on child sexual abuse, it is imperative to know the myths that exist surrounding the subject. Here are a few to take note of:

MYTH #1 - CHILD SEXUAL ABUSE IS ONLY EXECUTED BY STRANGERS.

This is a very common perception that is far from accurate. In fact, as mentioned above, 93% of children know their abuser. And with only 7% of abusers falling under the stranger category, it is crucial to understand the signs and behaviors to pick up cues from people who are around your children.

MYTH #2 - MANY CHILD SEXUAL ABUSE VICTIMS SPEAK UP ABOUT THE ABUSE.

According to *Darkness to Light*, it is estimated that around 73% of child sexual abuse victims do not mention the abuse for at least one year. Additionally, up to 45% of victims will not speak of the abuse for up to five years, with some never disclosing what happened. Although there are almost 80,000 reports of sexual abuse annually, the actual number that should be reported is in fact far greater, but many will not speak up because they are afraid or feel ashamed.

MYTH #3 - ONLY GIRLS ARE SEXUALLY ABUSED.

While women are more likely to be abused, men are also sexually abused. According to the National Institute of Health, the proportion of female sexual abuse during childhood ranges between 25% and 33%, with estimates for men ranging between 10% and 16%.

MYTH #4 - SEXUAL ABUSE IN FAMILIES IS USUALLY A ONE-TIME INCIDENT.

According to the World Health Organization, sexual abuse which occurs in the home typically transpires over time and occurs repeatedly.

MYTH #5 - FAMILY CHILD SEXUAL ABUSE ONLY HAPPENS IN LOW-INCOME HOUSEHOLDS.

Boys and girls from all race groups and social classes can be victims of sexual abuse. Perpetrators come from low, middle, and high-income households.

MYTH #6 - SEXUAL INTERACTIONS THAT AREN'T VIOLENT BETWEEN A CHILD AND AN ADULT WILL NOT DAMAGE THE CHILD.

According to the American Academy of Child and Adolescent Psychiatry, sexual abuse of any kind can result in lasting emotional and psychological damage. Victims typically struggle with feelings of shame, guilt, anger, and confusion. In addition, victims grow into adulthood with low self-esteem, and have a higher likelihood of being revictimized, and of experiencing depression, suicidal thoughts, or the desire to self-harm.

02

WHY DO WE NEED SEXUAL ABUSE TRAINING?

To gain a better understanding of child sexual abuse, we will look at the types of sexual abuse, symptoms, signs, behaviors of abusers, who to call for help, and how to report abuse.

Opportunities to prevent child abuse are frequently missed because of the lack of knowledge and misinformation on the topic. Although society as a whole has begun to acknowledge the scope of child sexual abuse and how much it is harming our children, we can and must do better.

PARENTS AND EDUCATORS NEED TO RECOGNIZE AND RESPOND TO THE BEHAVIORS AND SYMPTOMS OF SEXUAL ABUSE.

Children need to be taught to speak openly if someone behaves in a sexual way towards them. And we must know the correct steps to take if we believe someone is sexually interested in a child or harming a child in any way.

People who sexually abuse children are often those we know well and care about. It could be a mother, father, step-parent, grandparent, or other family members. The abuser could also be a baby-sitter, neighbor, coach, teacher, clergy member, or anyone else who is close to the child. Child sexual abuse occurs in all ethnic groups and has no regard for social class, race, religious affiliation, or sexual orientation.

Discussing the topic of sex is not easy at times, and speaking about child sexual abuse can be even more difficult, but not talking openly about this topic can have devastating consequences. It may be hard to believe or fathom that someone we know might view children sexually and desire to abuse them. And while we may not fully understand it, we can do something to prevent and stop it by identifying and recognizing the behaviors and signs.

03

WHY DO PEOPLE SEXUALLY ABUSE?

A question frequently asked is: "Why do people sexually abuse children?" There is not a straightforward answer to this question. Every person who abuses a child in this way is motivated to do so by their own unique issues.

Some people are primarily attracted to children. Some people, who are attracted to adults, may sexually approach a child during times of unusual stress like a divorce or job loss. And there are also some people who sexually abuse a child because they themselves were victims of sexual abuse or neglect. This, however, is not to be viewed as an excuse, but rather as factual insight. Keep in mind that while those who have been sexually abused as children have a higher chance of abusing a child later on in life, the majority live out their lives without harming anyone.

In some cases of child sexual abuse, the act is an impulsive one and occurs when an unexpected opportunity with a child presents itself. Sometimes, an adult will sexually abuse a child to feel power or control that they are not feeling in other relationships or areas of their life. These are a few examples of why someone may abuse a child. None of these reasons justify any sexual behavior involving a child. No matter what reason or excuse the abuser states for abusing a child, the child is the one who suffers from lasting effects that can be severe and linger throughout his or her life.

ADULTS WHO SEXUALLY ABUSE

While we discussed why some people sexually abuse children, it is also important to add that abusers rely on confusion and peoples' reluctance to acknowledge discomfort to get away with their crime.

Trusting your gut and instincts is crucial when it comes to abuse. If something doesn't seem right, speak up. If you feel uncomfortable but don't see specific signs, ask questions and keep an eye out for the following behavior:

- Makes others uncomfortable by ignoring emotional, physical, or social boundaries and limits.

- Refuses to let a child set his or her own limit.

- Teases or belittles a child to keep the child from setting his or her own limits.

- Makes sexual references or tells sexual jokes when children are present.

- Exposes children to adult sexual interactions without apparent concern.

- Has secret interactions with children or teens.

- Spends excessive time texting, emailing, or calling children or young people.

- Babysits children often for free or takes children out on special outings alone.

CHILDREN WHO SEXUALLY ABUSE

In addition to adults who sexually abuse, there are also children who sexually abuse, or peer-to-peer abuse. When children or preteens sexually interact with one another, it can be hard to tell the difference between natural sexual curiosity and abusive behavior. Young children who engage in inappropriate sexual interactions with their peers do not understand the impact it will have on themselves and others. However, some interactions between peers should raise concern regarding sexual abuse. If you witness something involving sexual behavior that has you questioning abuse, consider:

- **SIZE** - Is there a significant size or strength difference between the children/teens?

- **STATUS** - Does one of the teens or children have more status or power than the other? For example, is one of the children involved the babysitter, team leader, or a popular child who bullies?

- **POWER** - Are threats, tricks, bribes, or physical force being used against one of the teens or children?

- **ABILITY** - Is there a significant difference in the mental, physical, or emotional abilities of the children or teens? Is the potential victim developmentally delayed or disabled?

AGE-APPROPRIATE
SEXUAL BEHAVIOR TIPS

—

Talking to children about sexual development and their bodies can be intimidating and difficult. At a very young age, children begin to explore their bodies by touching, poking, pulling, and rubbing their body parts, including their genitals. As children grow older, it is critical that they are guided in learning about these body parts and their functions.

WHAT'S NORMAL WHAT'S NOT NORMAL

| 0-5 YEARS OF AGE

APPROPRIATE: Sexual language regarding differences in body parts, birth, pregnancy, and using the bathroom. Showing or looking at body parts. Genital stimulation.

INAPPROPRIATE: Displaying explicit sexual behavior or discussing specific sexual acts. Displaying adult-like sexual contact with other children.

| 6 – 12 YEARS OF AGE

APPROPRIATE BEFORE PUBERTY: Questioning relationships and sexual behavior. Experimenting with same-age children, typically during games, touching, kissing, and role-playing. Private genital stimulation.

INAPPROPRIATE BEFORE PUBERTY: Adult-like sexual interactions, public genital stimulation, discussing specific adult sexual acts.

APPROPRIATE AFTER PUBERTY: Increased curiosity about sex, questioning relationships, and sexual behavior. Using sexual words and phrases, talking about sex with peers. Experimenting with open mouth kissing and fondling. Masturbating while alone.

INAPPROPRIATE AFTER PUBERTY: Continuous adult-like sexual behavior, oral/genital contact or intercourse.

| 13 – 16 YEARS OF AGE

APPROPRIATE: Questioning sexual customs and social relationships. Masturbating while alone. Experimenting with same-age peers, fondling, etc. Intercourse occurs in 1/3 of this age group.

INAPPROPRIATE: Masturbating in public. Showing sexual interest in younger children.

04

PATTERNS OF SEXUAL ABUSE OFFENDERS

"The serial killer has the same personality characteristics as the sex offender against children."
-Dr. Mace Knapp, Nevada State Prison Psychologist

Now that you are more aware that child sexual abuse can happen to both boys and girls of any age and socioeconomic background, and in most cases is carried out by someone the victim knows, it is crucial to understand the patterns, habits, and behaviors of a sexual abuse offender.

According to The National Center for Missing & Exploited Children, there are more than 740,000 sexual offenders living in the United States – and these numbers only refer to those who are registered. Some have fallen off the radar, unable to be tracked!

It isn't uncommon for child predators to stalk their victims beforehand and learn their routine. To accomplish this, they may move near a child's school or park, or become employed in a location that has regular access to children. For some sexual predators such as pedophiles, the urge to have sex with a child, is described as irresistible, and according to Sex-offenders.us, it is estimated that pedophiles molest an average of 260 children during their lifetime.

Child sexual abuse offenders follow a specific grooming process when it comes to victims. Here are common behavior patterns to be aware of:

1. **IDENTIFYING AND TARGETING::** The first step in reaching their goal to victimize a child is to identify and target a child, and in some cases, his or her caregivers as well. Offenders will often seek defenseless children with vulnerable parents.

2. **GAINING TRUST & ACCESS:** When a child has been identified, it will be time for the offender to gain his or her trust, which will allow access to the child. For some offenders, they will learn what activities a child likes, follow his or her play activity or schedule, give them rides to activities, and provide them with gifts or treats that they love. For other victims, the offender may act as a trusted friend, someone who offers a sympathetic ear, and provides particular attention to the child.

3. **ISOLATING THE CHILD IN SOME WAY:** Isolation is vital to the offender in order for there to be opportunities to victimize the child. In the majority of cases, the offender was able to get the child alone, gain access in some way, or manipulate relationships to create scenarios where he or she is alone with the child. In some cases, however, sexual abuse has taken place while other adults were in the room, but the abuser and the abuse somehow was able to take place undetected.

4. **PLAYING A ROLE:** Child sexual offenders typically use manipulative tactics to play a role in a child's life. These tactics can take the form of being empathetic to the child and making him or her feel like the offender is the only person who "understands" them or vice versa. This type of manipulation can lead the child to believe this relationship is unique and can only be filled by the offender. Predators are experts at finding weak spots in children and using that knowledge to make their relationship seem different than others.

    - **THE AFFECTION LURE** – Keep in mind the "Affection Lure" is commonly used by predators online and in-person to exploit unsuspecting victims who are seeking love and attention. Years of research and interviews have revealed that child molesters consistently seek out children who have a physically or emotionally absent parent, and will spend hours, days, weeks, or months grooming the child through this vulnerability.

5. **CREATING A SECRET RELATIONSHIP:** To prevent anyone from learning about the abuse, the offender must coerce the child in some way to keep him or her from sharing details of the relationship. This can be accomplished through telling the child that no one would understand their relationship, or they may not approve of it, or it can be through a variety of threats such as physical harm to the child or his or her family, suicide, or some other type of traumatic repercussion.

6. **INTRODUCING SEXUAL CONTACT:** Once a child sexual abuse offender believes he or she has successfully completed the above steps, the abuse can be initiated. Initial physical contact can be a pat on the shoulder or holding of hands. This can gradually progress to more sexually-charged actions. This slow progress of physical touch can diminish the child's reservations and desensitize him or her over time.

7. **BEING IN CONTROL OF THE RELATIONSHIP:** For the abuse to continue, the offender must stay in control of the relationship. This may be accomplished by telling the child no one will believe them if they come forward, or that the child's actions are the cause of the abuse. Creating fear or shame in the child can keep the child from speaking out in many abuse situations.

CHILD SEXUAL ABUSE OFFENDERS AND GAINING ACCESS

While we now know a little more about the tactics and methods child molesters use to identify and control their victims, you might be wondering where they find children to exploit. Here are some of the most common ways offenders gain access to children:

- Becoming a foster or guardian parent
- Offering to provide coaching services for children's sporting events
- Attending children's sporting events
- Befriending parents, especially those who are single or separated
- Offering to babysit
- Taking a job or volunteering at community events that engage children
- Offering to be a chaperone on overnight trips that involve children
- Volunteering at youth organizations, camps, etc.
- Spending time at popular hangouts for children such as playgrounds, parks, arcades, malls, pools, baseball fields, skate parks, etc.
- Creating profiles on social media and game platforms (in which many will pretend to be a minor themselves)

| FINDING SPECIFIC TARGETS

Though we briefly touched on the fact that predators look for children who have an emotionally or physically absent guardian or parent, there are many other tactics used by offenders to secure a target.

Whether the offender is interacting with the minor online or in-person, early grooming efforts commence in which the offender determines how secure the home life of the child is. Abusers specifically look for children who face challenges within their home life e.g., divorce, poverty, illness, drug abuse, and homelessness.

Children who are considered loners, neglected, or troubled are also highly targeted. Kids who regularly smoke, drink alcohol, or use drugs are often seen as unsupervised and more accessible targets. Single mothers are also a popular target among abusers, as they can often be overwhelmed with career and family duties. In this type of scenario, an abuser may offer to drive the child to school or extracurricular activities, or offer to babysit while the parent is at work.

THE THREE TYPES OF SEXUAL PREDATORS

—

Child sexual abuse offenders will fall into one or more of the categories below. Though each type of offender comes with specific behaviors and preferences, the common thread between all types is their lack of conscience. Each type is dangerous to children at all times.

PEDOPHILES

Pedophiles are men or women who have a sexual preference for children and no interest in having sexual relationships with adults. Pedophiles become criminals when they act upon this desire, whether it is having sex with a child, paying for child pornography, etc.

PREFERENTIAL ABUSERS

Preferential abusers have a "preference" towards children, most commonly of pre-pubescent age. The majority of these abusers are male (though some are female), and they have ongoing, specific patterns of choosing a target and grooming the child before initiating sexual contact.

SITUATIONAL ABUSERS

This type of offender relies on specific opportunities or situations to arise. He or she enjoys sex with both adults and children and will often victimize if the "opportunity" arises. This "opportunity" could be a child left alone, the offender being drunk, the offender wanting to hurt/get even with the child's parents, etc.

Researchers have extensively studied biological, personality, and cognitive theories as to why child sexual offenders carry out these acts against children. Though some studies have recognized abnormalities in the brains of some offenders, these abnormalities do not exist in the majority of cases (Aigner et al., 2000; Corley et al., 1994; Galski, Thornton, & Shumsky, 1990). Regarding personality and cognitive theories, research has yielded numerous behaviors and thinking patterns seen in child sexual abusers. Here are a few to be aware of:

- They often diminish any feelings of shame and guilt.
- They will make excuses for their behavior.
- They will often minimize the extent of harm done.
- They might claim they are entitled to their behavior.
- They might blame the victim or see them as deserving of the abuse.
- They usually have poor relationships with others.
- They have low self-esteem.
- When confronted about their behavior, they will reframe the situation to preserve their image.
- They tend to blame others or diminish personal responsibility.
- Research in male abusers has found they have not developed the social skills, self-confidence, and quality attachments to form effective intimate relationships with their peers.

SEXUAL ABUSERS AND RED FLAG OFFENSES

With the knowledge that over 90 percent of child sexual abuse cases involve someone the child knows, it is critical to know red flag behaviors to look out for when observing people around your child. Red flag offenses include:

1. **"PEEPING TOM"** – This includes someone who regularly walks in on a minor changing or using the restroom or shower, or who has an interest in watching a child carry out these behaviors from afar.

2. **PROVIDING SUBSTANCES TO A CHILD** – With this behavior, the offender may provide alcohol, cigarettes, or drugs to the minor to gain his or her trust or to begin to build a secret relationship they will later use to control the child.

3. **PROVIDING PORNOGRAPHY TO A MINOR** – Though pornography is readily available today with just a few clicks on the Internet, providing this material to a child under 18 is a crime. This can come in the form of books, magazines, pictures, drawings, movies, or other types of recorded video, and delivery of the items can be electronically or in-person. Offenders may do this for a variety of reasons: as part of the grooming process or to create a secret element to the relationship they have with the victim.

4. **FLASHING** – Flashing, like providing pornography to a minor, is considered a non-contact form of sexual abuse and needs to be reported.

5. **STALKING** – Stalking is a serious crime, and in some cases can escalate or turn violent over time. It is estimated that 7.5 million people are stalked every year in the United States. Behaviors of stalking include: the individual showing up where the minor is; sending a child unwanted gifts, letters, or emails; using technology like GPS or hidden cameras to keep tabs on a child; driving by the child's home or school; or threatening to hurt the child's family, friends, or pets.

6. **ENGAGING IN FREQUENT PHYSICAL CONTACT WITH A MINOR** – Other red flags include an offender constantly seeking out reasons to touch a child anywhere on their body. For example, an offender could continually ask a child to sit on their lap or always ask the child for hugs or kisses.

THE
ABUSER:
A PERSON YOU
WOULD NEVER
EXPECT

Without proper education, parents or guardians might make the mistake of believing strangers are the people to worry about when it comes to the potential victimization of their children, but statistics clearly show this is not the case. Below are a variety of profiles of sex offenders and more about their crimes. These people include teachers, camp counselors, court-appointed guardians, and other people with access to children.

PETER NEWMAN

Peter Newman worked as an assistant director and camp counselor for Kanakuk Kamps for 10 years. During this time, he preyed on and groomed young boys, especially those between the ages of 11 and 15. He would invite them over for Bible studies in his home where court records showed activities such as skinny-dipping in his hot tub, playing nude basketball, and sleep-overs that included molestation taking place. He is now serving 35 years for the molestations he committed against young boys at this camp.

JENNIFER RICE

Jennifer Rice is a former Tacoma schoolteacher and mother of three children who was sentenced for 25 years to life for having sex with her 10-year-old student on multiple occasions, as well as his 15-year-old brother. Rice was convicted of first-degree kidnapping, first-degree child molestation, and two counts of third-degree rape. The judge presiding over the case found the molestation and kidnapping charges were predatory offenses – this designation is mandatory when a teacher is charged with sex crimes and comes with stiffer sentencing requirements.

JOE BARRON

Joe Barron is a former minister who pleaded guilty and received a seven-year prison term for soliciting sex with a 13-year-old girl online. Barron chatted for several weeks with the "girl" (an undercover officer) online and requested she skip school to meet with him. When arrested, he was found carrying 10 condoms and a camera as a gift for the young girl.

ABIGAIL ANNE HOLLOWAY

Abigail Holloway is a former private school softball coach who engaged in a sexual relationship for three years with a student who was 13 years old at the time their relationship began. She was arrested on 15 counts of child molestations and sex perversion.

BILLY DAN CARROLL

Billy Dan Carroll was a court-appointed child advocate who was arrested after police seized videos of him having sex with children. These events included sex with a seven-year-old girl, sexually assaulting a 6-year-old on 23 occasions, a 2-year-old on five occasions, and taping a 13-year-old girl through a hidden video camera in his bathroom. As a court-appointed advocate, Carroll's job was to get to know the abused children he was assigned to, and to work alongside their family, teachers, physicians and the courts. He was sentenced to life in prison plus forty years.

SYMPTOMS OF SEXUAL ABUSE
WHAT ARE YOUR NEXT STEPS FOR REPORTING

So what happens when someone fails to report abuse or fails to report it promptly? Let's take a look at a 2012 news story involving an Oklahoma church. In 2012, two men were hired as janitors at Victory Christian Church in Tulsa, OK. One man allegedly raped a 13-year-old girl during one of the services, and the other man reportedly propositioned a 15-year-old girl to send nude photos, in addition to sending her lewd messages through social media. Both men were eventually arrested, but it took members of the church (who were told of the incidents immediately) several weeks to contact authorities. Because of this lapse in contacting the police, five staff members from the church were also arrested and criminally charged with failure to report sexual abuse.

So how can you determine if someone is being sexually abused? Consider the following common signs and behaviors:

BEHAVIORAL SYMPTOMS OF SEXUAL ABUSE

- Nightmares and/or sleeping issues
- Extreme fear without an obvious explanation
- An older child exhibiting sudden younger child behaviors such as thumb-sucking
- Sudden personality changes, seeming angry, withdrawn, clingy, moody, "checked-out"
- Fear of being in certain places or around certain people for unknown reasons
- Resistance to being alone with a specific person
- Resistance to removing clothes to bathe or use the bathroom in appropriate situations
- Writing, drawing, or dreaming of sexual or frightening images
- Refusal to share a secret he/she has with an adult
- Illness or stomach ache with no identifiable reason
- Using new or adult words for body parts
- Intentionally harming or hurting him or herself with drugs, cutting, burning, alcohol, running away, etc.
- Engaging in adult-like sexual activity with toys, objects, or other children

05

Whether you suspect abuse is taking place or have concrete evidence, you might be wondering where and how to report it, and what the laws are surrounding child sexual abuse. Let's take a look at more information regarding the laws and your responsibility to report the situation.

Laws mandate that any person who knows or has reasonable cause to suspect child abuse, neglect or abandonment shall immediately report this knowledge to the Department of Children and Families and/or the police. Also, any person with this knowledge who fails to report child abuse, neglect, or abandonment can be charged with a misdemeanor or felony, depending on the state in which they preside. Each state also designates people with specific career positions (doctors, nurses, counselors, etc.) as "mandatory reporters," who must tell officials immediately if child abuse is suspected.

PHYSICAL SYMPTOMS OF SEXUAL ABUSE

- Pain, discoloration, bleeding or discharge in genitals, anus, or mouth.
- Persistent or recurring pain during urination or bowel movements.
- Wetting or soiling accidents unrelated to potty training.
- Sexually transmitted disease.
- Pregnancy.

SYMPTOMS OF NEGLECT

- Clothes that are dirty, ill-fitting, or inappropriate for the weather.
- Consistently bad hygiene, such as being unbathed, having dirty or matted hair, or body odor.
- Untreated physical injuries or illness.
- Frequently being unsupervised or left alone to play in unsafe environments.
- Frequently being late or missing from school.

SYMPTOMS OF PHYSICAL ABUSE

- Frequent injuries or unexplained bruises, cuts, or welts.
- Displaying watchful behavior or always being on alert.
- Injuries displaying a pattern from a hand or belt.
- Shying away from touch or being afraid to go home.
- Wearing inappropriate clothing to cover injuries.

06

HOW TO PREVENT SEXUAL ABUSE

And Where Do You Start?

Unfortunately, child sexual abuse and sexual assault are usually discussed when it is too late, diminishing the possibility of preventing the abuse. Teaching your child about sexual abuse should be a part of your basic safety plan and information. Just like certain rules and information change as a child grows - such as "look both ways before crossing the road" or "do not play near a street" - your child's understanding of sexual abuse can increase as he or she matures. Basic rules should be taught early and in a positive style.

All children should have a basic working vocabulary for all body parts, not just eyes, ears, nose, toes, etc. Even though these words are often taught to children less than one-year-old, words for the child's genital, breast, and anal areas are not typically discussed. Not having acceptable names for those areas on the body can give the impression to your child that it is not okay to talk about those body parts. Without proper names, it will be impossible to discuss sexual abuse and assault.

You are your child's first teacher. Knowing the correct names for genitalia enhances your child's respect for his or her body. Imagine the impact on your child if the first time he or she is exposed to the words penis or vagina is through the media or peers. This could create confusion, misinformation, and potentially cause issues.

TEACH YOUR CHILD TO USE THEIR WORDS

Teach your child to use his or her words if someone is inappropriately touching them, tickling them, or forcing unwanted touch upon them. Potential phrases to teach could be something like:

- "You are not allowed to touch me."
- "No, do not touch me with your penis/vagina."
- "No, do not make me touch your penis/vagina."
- "Do not touch my bottom."

TIPS TO PREVENT SEXUAL ABUSE

- Show interest in a child's day-to-day life.
- Familiarize yourself with people in your child's life.
- Choose babysitters and other caregivers carefully.
- Talk about the media openly.
- Teach your child the names of his or her body parts.
- Teach children early and often that there are no secrets between adults and children.
- Learn the behavioral and physical warning signs of sexual abuse.
- Teach your child it is okay to speak up.
- Teach your child about having boundaries.
- Be available and willing to listen and/or talk.
- Reassure them they will not get in trouble.
- Give them a chance to talk about new topics.
- Create an environment in your home where sexual topics can be discussed.

In addition to teaching our children about safety, it is crucial to educate ourselves as much as possible and actively keep up with changes in technology. The following tips can help you create a family plan for safety and also offer advice on how to keep your home pornography free.

PRACTICAL WAYS TO PREVENT SEXUAL ABUSE

STAY ALERT FOR INAPPROPRIATE BEHAVIORS: Be sure to keep an eye out for inappropriate behavior or contact with adults or older children, particularly when it comes to young children. Younger children might not be as cognizant to these behaviors and are subsequently less able to protect themselves. Make it a point to know what your child is viewing on iPhones, tablets, iPads, and computers not just when they are at home, but also at friends' houses.

BE AWARE OF INTERNET USAGE IN CHILDREN: Stay abreast of your child's usage of and interactions via email, webcams, instant messaging, social networking sites, peer-to-peer sites, cell phone, and picture exchanges. Model appropriate behavior to your child regarding these outlets and vocalize precautions you take. Keep all interactions via these outlets public and visible. This visibility can prevent dangerous or inappropriate situations from occurring. Establish firm, clear guidelines regarding the internet and cell phone usage and stick to these guidelines. If there is a violation of the clearly stated boundaries, make sure your child knows there will be specific consequences.

ESTABLISH AND RESPECT ALL FAMILY BOUNDARIES: Each member of the family has the right to bathe, sleep, and dress in privacy. If anyone is disrespecting the boundaries you have set within your family, an adult should remind them of the rules that have been put in place.

TEACH YOUR CHILDREN THE IMPORTANCE OF SAYING "NO": It is crucial for children to understand and believe their "No" will be respected. If they are being tickled, kissed, hugged, experiencing any type of unwanted touch, or being shown images that make them feel uneasy they should reply with a firm, "No!" This "No" should be respected, even in seemingly innocent cases. Be sure to keep all family members on board regarding this rule since it benefits the overall safety of the family.

SAY SOMETHING WHEN WITNESSING INAPPROPRIATE BEHAVIOR: If you witness inappropriate behavior, interrupt and speak up to whomever is making you or your child uncomfortable. If this isn't possible, speak to someone who is in a position to intervene. The individual may need professional help to stop these inappropriate behaviors.

REPORT ANY SEXUAL ABUSE: If you suspect or know any sexual abuse is occurring, report it immediately. If someone does not speak up for the victim, the abuse will never stop.

SAFETY PLAN FOR YOUR FAMILY ADAPTED FROM "THE PORN FREE FAMILY PLAN" BY CHALLIES.COM, AND STOP IT NOW!

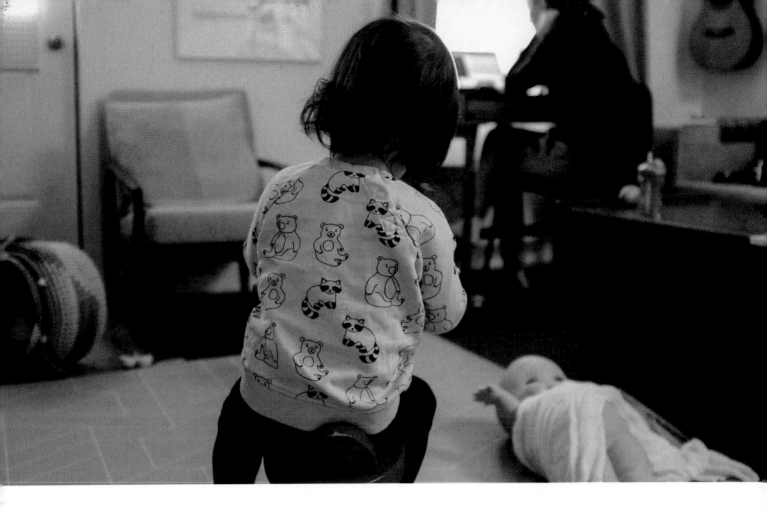

HOW TO SELECT CAREGIVERS, BABYSITTERS AND DAY CARES

As a parent, it can be overwhelming to think about how you could ever trust anyone to take care of your child and prioritize their safety as much as you do. Whether its an extra shift at work or date night, you will eventually have to introduce a caregiver into your child's life. But how can you find someone who will be genuinely dedicated to your child's safety and happiness? When the time comes to give someone that direct access to your child, we want to help you develop the most thorough screening process to strengthen any vulnerabilities and lower the risk of your child being sexually abused.

FOLLOW UP WITH THEIR REFERENCES
It's important to require a minimum of 3 references so you can attain several different perspectives about the applicant. The best references are people you already know and whose judgment you trust such as your friends, family members, or co-workers who have hired that applicant. Follow through with their references and ask questions such as "What was their interaction style with your children?", "Why do they no longer work for you?", and "Would you rehire them?".

BACKGROUND CHECKS
You want to always treat a person who is going to be around your child like a person you are going to hire. You want to conduct a background check and research public records.

INTERVIEW THEM IN PERSON

this gives you a chance to personally analyze how the caregiver would handle different real-life scenarios and how they would get along with your child. Don't be afraid to ask as many necessary questions as needed to ensure your child will be in good hands.

CHECK THEIR SOCIAL MEDIA
In addition to a professional background check, looking at their social media gives you further insight into their daily life and personality. Does the content they post align with your values? Are there any red flags in their pictures, posts, or comments? Ask them about any concerning information you find.

UNEXPECTED CHECK-INS
Once they are hired, drop in unexpectedly without notice so they understand that you are active and engaged in your child's safety. Knowing that you are keeping a watchful eye over them could encourage the caregiver to follow your rules, uphold safety boundaries, and do a better job overall.

SET UP CAMERAS IN YOUR HOUSEHOLD
Having an additional form of monitoring your child when you aren't physically there can help decrease the risk of sexual abuse from happening within your household. Along with traditional home surveillance devices, there are also cameras that include mobile software so you can have a live stream and easily check in on your child from your phone.

AVOID HIRING OLDER CHILDREN OR TEENAGERS

If they are still young enough to be dependent on their own parents, they should not be taking care of your child. It's also important to remember that child on child sexual abuse occurs more often than people believe, so it's safer to hire a professional caregiver.

WHEN SELECTING DAY CARES FOR YOUR CHILD

It's important to take your time and to be thorough when hiring a day care center to look after your child. Don't concern yourself with looking like a helicopter parent when researching if a specific day care is right for your family. Here are some simple steps we recommend when evaluating day cares:

- Read online reviews.

- Tour the day care and watch how children interact.

- Look for children not being monitored by adults.

- Ask about their policy on who (parents, other children, cleaning people, maintenance workers, etc.) may come into the day care and come in contact with children.

- Have all staff such as cleaners, maintenance workers, teachers, substitutes, assistants, etc. been background checked?

- If your day care is at a person's home, what other family members are allowed in the home? Have they been background checked?

- Drop in on occasion unannounced.

- Ask where cameras are and request to see what they record so you can check if there are any hidden spots in the day care or home that are not being recorded.

As a parent, it is your job to set clear boundaries for the people who provide care for your children. You want to set age-appropriate rules for day cares and caregivers and then talk to your child about those rules, why their caregiver or day care has to follow them, how to uphold them, and how to speak up if those rules are broken. Body safety boundaries and clear rules of interaction will decrease the amount of opportunities someone at the day care or a caregiver gets to use their authoritative power to take advantage of your child. Additional rules such as determining how much time is appropriate to spend online or using technology and stating that anyone visiting must be approved by a parent in advance can also be helpful in lessening vulnerabilities to sexual abuse. Remember that prevention is the most powerful tool a parent can use to protect a child from sexual abuse.

07
INTERNET SAFETY

Communication has drastically changed over the years, and now more than ever most communication is being completed using cell phones. Even young children and teenagers rely more on their phone to communicate than any other electronic device. A recent study from Ofcom.com shared that among kids aged 12 – 15, 34% state their smartphone is their main device for sending or posting messages to other people.

In addition to smartphones, tablets have also become another widely used device for children and young people, thanks to their ease of use and the popularity of gaming among children (performed primarily on tablets).

So, what steps can parents take to keep their children safe from online sexual predators who might try to communicate via cell phone or tablet? There are many steps that can be take, such as verbal communication with your children, filters, safety programs, etc.

First, it is important for parents to understand there are different types of online risks that have the potential to harm their children. Here are three to be aware of:

| CONTENT RISK

Searching online or interacting with the Internet on a cell phone or tablet always involves "content risk." This means children could find mass-distributed content such as pornography, violence, hate speech, etc.

| CONDUCT RISK

With conduct risk, children are participating with an interactive program. This could be messaging an unknown person and engaging in sexting, over-sharing, sending personal information, or being harassed, intimidated or bullied online.

| CONTACT RISK

In this category, children are now victims of the interactive situation. This could mean meeting a stranger they met online, being stalked or harassed, having personal photos or their house address shared online, having their privacy compromised, or being intimidated or bullied.

Because of the dangers that are present with online activity, whether it is on a smartphone or tablet, parents can take the following steps to help prevent their child from becoming a victim.

1. **CONSIDER PARENTAL CONTROLS** – Many programs are available that allow parents to control what their children are seeing or even when they can access the Internet. For instance, if your child enjoys watching YouTube videos, there is a parental control panel located on the site that will allow you to filter out certain types of videos.

    In addition, you might want to consider the Covenant Eyes Filter. This filter allows you to choose when the Internet can be accessed, how much time your child is allotted for the Internet each week, and can also block certain websites, instant messaging, file sharing, etc.

2. **TEACH PROTECTION TIPS** – Teach children to protect themselves online regarding their personal information, photos, and/or situations they might be experiencing. Explain how posting certain content such as pictures or information can be taken by a sexual predator and used for ways not originally intended.

    In addition, discuss the dangers of speaking to strangers in chat rooms, in gaming forums, on Facebook, etc. and how these strangers may misrepresent themselves as someone their age in order to take their guard down. Remember, it is not uncommon for online predators to create comprehensive fake profiles of themselves using someone else's pictures and information.

3. **COMMUNICATE!** – Have open dialogue with your children and tell them to inform you immediately if someone they do not know is asking for personal information, photos, or wants to meet in "real life."

https://www.safesearchkids.com/cell-phone-safety-tips-for-tweens-and-teens/#.W0dcDNhKiRs

https://assets.publishing.service.gov.uk/government/uploads/system/uploads/attachment_data/file/487973/ukccis_guide-final_3_.pdf

http://www.pbs.org/parents/expert-tips-advice/2018/01/online-safety-tips-parents-young-children/

EXPOSURE TO INAPPROPRIATE CONTENT

Even if your child is browsing the internet for something as innocent as homework information or tutorials, any site can become a gateway site that exposes your child to inappropriate content with a single click. A protective strategy for accessing the internet is to enable Safe Browsing through your browser settings. This allows additional security against potential online threats, unsafe sites and password breaches through your search engine.

For further privacy settings in a social media capacity, check for the "Privacy" tab in the "Settings" section of each of the applications your child uses such as Facebook, YouTube, Instagram, Twitter, Snapchat, Twitch, and TikTok. Social media sites and applications often offer user-friendly privacy settings to determine who can see your child's profile and posts, who can message them, and what type of content they are exposed to.

Sites such as www.internetmatters.org/parental-controls are helpful prevention tools for parents regarding privacy and security controls, as they allow you to select specific types of devices, websites, entertainment streaming services, social media sites, and gaming software for detailed information on setting up parental controls and monitoring your child's activity and exposure.

It is inevitable that your child will see inappropriate content at some point in their youth. As a parent, you can prepare them for that moment in the following ways:

- Let them know that they can immediately tell you if they see any inappropriate content. Remind them that if they are honest with you, you will not judge their actions but rather talk about what happened and how to avoid it happening again.
- Blocking can be a powerful safety tool! Guide your child on how to block messages or requests from unknown or unsafe profiles and users with each application that has chatting or follow features.
- Take some time to browse through streaming services like Netflix, Hulu, Twitch, and YouTube to determine what type of content, shows, movies, or channels are age-appropriate for them to watch.

Parental control settings on streaming and television services along with social media responses to removing flagged or reported content act as a safety net to avoiding exposure. However, the most reliable source of prevention comes from having conversations with your child about the harmful impact that exposure to inappropriate content can have on them and what digital safety measures can help keep them safe.

APP DOWNLOADS AND PURCHASES

For a child, apps have the ability to make their online world go round. Phone applications can provide access to games, social media, streaming services, the internet, and everything in between. One proactive digital prevention tool is to create your child's app store account under your family sharing group. This allows you to decrease online vulnerabilities by improving app management with necessary purchase agreements and application downloads to remain age-appropriate, digitally safe, and cost-effective.

PROTECTING PERSONAL INFORMATION

With ever-changing technology and endless access to the internet, children face an infinite web-space of vulnerabilities that can leave them exposed to online sexual abuse. Although every social media application, online gaming software, and streaming sites have their own gateways to abuse exposure, here are some general online safety practices you can talk to your child about to protect their personal information and safety:

"JUST AS YOUR BODY BELONGS TO YOU, SO DOES YOUR PRIVATE INFORMATION"

- Children should create private profiles with usernames that do not contain their entire name or picture.
- A great prevention strategy is to be part of the profile creation process as a parent, to have access to all the account information and have your child only use that specific account to avoid vulnerabilities while also giving you supervisory access.
- Children should avoid giving information or activating features that can be used to contact or locate them such as addresses, public location-sharing, geotags, school names, phone numbers, afterschool programs, or sports teams.

YOUR CHILD'S ONLINE SOCIAL CIRCLE SHOULD BE THE SAME AS THEIR SOCIAL CIRCLE IN REAL LIFE.

- If they receive a social media follow request or a player request to join a game from a stranger, or anyone they do not personally talk to or trust in their real life, they should avoid replying and let a parent or trusted adult know.
- Talk to your child about the dangers of catfishing. The internet is full of possibilities, but the reality is that one of those possibilities includes the danger behind an abuser pretending to be someone else via a fake profile.

HOW TO PROMOTE DIGITAL WELLBEING IN YOUR FAMILY

Technology is an incredible resource for learning, entertainment, and communication. Unfortunately, digital over-dependence can create issues of anxiety, low self-esteem, and peer pressure throughout a child's development. Here are some helpful tips for promoting digital wellbeing in your family and incorporating technology into your everyday life through healthy habits:

- Avoid device usage approximately 30 minutes to an hour before bedtime.
- Limit device usage during family gatherings such as sharing a meal together.
- Engage in weekly family check-ins to talk about social media, online sites, television, movies, and gaming software.
- Create a safe space for talking about any interesting, noteworthy, confusing, inappropriate, or discomforting content anyone might have been exposed to during the week.
- Be a role model! If your child sees you are constantly on your phone, they will most likely replicate that same behavior. Take some time during the day to promote device-free activities such as reading a book, playing outside, spending time with pets, and learning new hobbies.

08
SEXUAL ABUSE RESOURCES

NATIONAL SEXUAL ASSAULT HOTLINE:
National hotline, operated by RAINN, that serves people affected by sexual violence. It automatically routes the caller to their nearest sexual assault service provider. You can also search your local center here. Hotline: 800.656.HOPE

NATIONAL SEXUAL VIOLENCE RESOURCE CENTER:
This site offers a wide variety of information relating to sexual violence including a large legal resource library.

NATIONAL ORGANIZATION FOR VICTIM ASSISTANCE:
Founded in 1975, NOVA is the oldest national victim assistance organization of its type in the United States, and the recognized leader in this cause.

NATIONAL ONLINE RESOURCE CENTER ON VIOLENCE AGAINST WOMEN:
VAWnet, a project of the National Resource Center on Domestic Violence hosts a resource library which is home to thousands of materials on violence against women and related issues.

U.S. DEPARTMENT OF JUSTICE: NATIONAL SEX OFFENDER PUBLIC WEBSITE:
NSOPW is the only U.S. government website that links public state, territorial, and tribal sex offender registries from one national search site.

THE NATIONAL CENTER FOR VICTIMS OF CRIME:
The mission of the National Center for Victims of Crime is to forge a national commitment to help victims of crime rebuild their lives. They are dedicated to serving individuals, families, and communities harmed by crime.

NATIONAL CHILD ABUSE HOTLINE:
They can provide local referrals for services. A centralized call center provides the caller with the option of talking to a counselor. They are also connected to a language line that can provide services in over 140 languages. Hotline: 800.4.A.CHILD (422.2253)
CYBER TIPLINE:

This Tipline is operated by the National Center for Missing and Exploited Children. Can be used to communicate information to the authorities about child pornography or child sex trafficking. Hotline: 800.THE.LOST (843.5678)

NATIONAL CHILDREN'S ALLIANCE:
This organization represents the national network of Child Advocacy Centers (CAC). CACs are a multidisciplinary team of law enforcement and mental and physical health practitioners who investigate instances of child physical and sexual abuse. Their website explains the process and has a directory according to geographic location.

STOP IT NOW:
Provides information to victims and parents/relatives/friends of child sexual abuse. The site also has resources for offender treatment as well as information on recognizing the signs of child sexual abuse. Hotline: 888-PREVENT (773.8368)

JUSTICE FOR CHILDREN:
Provides a full range of advocacy services for abused and neglected children.

1 IN 6: FOR MEN SEXUALLY ABUSED AS CHILDREN:
Provides educational information and resources for men, family and friends, and professionals. Also provides access to the online hotline.

NANCY J. COTTERMAN CENTER:
If you or anyone you know need immediate help, contact the Nancy J. Cotterman Center on their 24-hour helpline at 954-761-RAPE (7273) or visit them online.

Made in the USA
Middletown, DE
08 May 2022

65480389R00024